Introduction

The quilt patterns in this book are intended for use to make fun and fabulous quilts for kids, but these same patterns can also be used to make wonderful lap quilts of all kinds. The sizes are perfect for cribs, laps and youth beds. One of these simple, but fun, fast and easy quilt patterns may be just what you are looking for.

This is a great book to have on hand. You never know when you may want to make a baby quilt or a small throw.

Any one of the projects in this book can easily be made by a beginner in a day or two. Many are perfect for the use of large focal fabrics that are just too pretty to cut into smaller pieces. These sweet designs will make you want to whip up a quilt this weekend.

If you have leftover fabrics from previous projects, here is an opportunity to also use them. Many of these designs may be used to make charity quilts. Do you have a special charity you quilt for? If so, many of the patterns will appeal to you. They are perfect for group quilting. If your guild is planning to host a charity-quilt day, these quilts can inspire the completion of many quilt tops in just one day.

The possibilities are endless. Thumb through this book with an open mind. You will be amazed at what you discover. ■

Meet the Designer

Connie Ewbank learned to embroider when she was in grade school, and how to crochet when she was in high school. She has tried and enjoyed many different crafts.

Connie made her first quilt for her sister who was expecting a baby. She's been making quilts ever since.

Connie owned a quilt and cross-stitch shop—Quilt N Stitch—in St. Louis, Mo., for 12 years. The shop offered lots of classes, many of them taught from designs created at the shop. Connie began to publish these designs in pattern and book form. She also purchased a separate counted–cross-stitch shop where she designed and taught classes.

In the early fall of 2004, Connie closed both shops and moved to the Baton Rouge, La., area. She has continued to teach and to design patterns for both quilting and counted cross-stitch. She publishes her cross-stitch designs under the name of Butterfly Stitches.

Teaching has taken Connie to many places around the Missouri, Ohio, Illinois and Kansas areas, and as far away as Monterrey, Mexico.

Since moving to Louisiana, she has expanded her teaching area  nd North Carolina. Connie has taught at local quilt guilds, local and regional a (EGA) meetings and local American Needlepoint Guild (ANG) meetings. ntains her pattern company. ■

House of White Birches, Berne, Indiana 4671

Charity Quilts

Fellow Quilters,

I can't think of a better way to spread the joy of quilting than to give a quilt to a child in need. There are so many worthy charities out there that finding just one to mention in this book was not an easy job. We did find a charity that we feel could benefit from this book and from the use of the patterns within. Quilts for Kids Inc. was founded in 2000 by Linda Arye, who was an interior designer at the time. Linda had a love of fabric and was interested in working with fabric companies to take their discontinued fabric samples, overruns and seconds, and turn them into quilts that would comfort children in need. Linda's daughter Mollie had survived two near-death experiences, and Linda knew how hard it was to spend countless hours in a hospital with a child. This is the experience that spurred Linda on to create Quilts for Kids.

Gifting quilts to children that they could keep forever was her inspiration for this charity. They were to be forever quilts—quilts the children could keep through their hospital stay and take home.

Quilts for Kids has stayed true to its founding ideas. It has also expanded to include children of abuse. In 2010, Quilts for Kids donated nearly 30,000 quilts to children fighting a lifelong battle with an illness and to children of abuse. With nearly 145,000 quilts donated to date, you can imagine the outpouring of loving quilters who have helped turn tears of pain into smiles. You could be one of them.

With more than six million children hospitalized in the United States alone, the need for quilts is huge. Quilts for Kids makes kits to send out to quilters, but it isn't enough. They ask quilters who receive the kits to make one or more quilts of their own so they can double or triple the number of children to whom they gift quilts.

If you're interested in helping a child in need, you can use a pattern from this book and visit www.quiltsforkids.org to get all the information. Quilters have big hearts, and this is one way to share your talents as a quilter. Use your stash to make a quilt for a child in need.

Quilts for Kids Mission Statement

Transforming discontinued, unwanted and other fabrics into patchwork quilts that comfort children with life-threatening illnesses and children of abuse.

Our hope is that you find this book an inspiration to make and donate a quilt to a child in need, whether it is for this charity or for one of your choosing. Make a child's day a little brighter with a quilt. ■

Acknowledgments

Several quilts in this book were professionally machine-quilted by Carol Hilton on her long-arm machine. Thank you, Carol, for making time in your busy schedule to quilt the Sweet & Simple Sampler (page 3) and Here's My Heart (page 12) quilts. They are beautiful! Thank you also to those of you who helped me stitch and bind a few of the quilts when I was overwhelmed.

Sweet & Simple Sampler

This is a sampler of many of the blocks used in this book. A sampler can be fascinating to make. Your fabric choices can make it perfect for a child or grandma's favorite.

Project Specifications
Skill Level: Beginner
Quilt Size: 50" x 56"
Block Size: 6" x 6"
Number of Blocks: 56

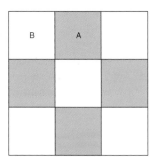

Nine-Patch
6" x 6" Block
Make 8

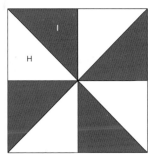

Pinwheel
6" x 6" Block
Make 8

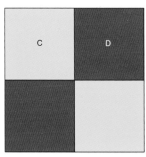

Yellow Four-Patch
6" x 6" Block
Make 2

Half-Square Triangle
6" x 6" Block
Make 10

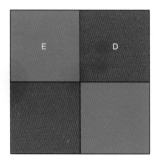

Green Four-Patch
6" x 6" Block
Make 6

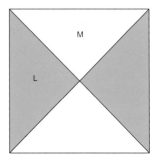

Hourglass
6" x 6" Block
Make 8

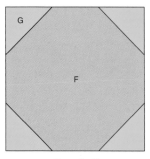

Snowball
6" x 6" Block
Make 6

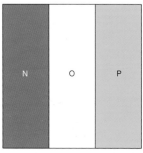

Rail Fence
6" x 6" Block
Make 8

Materials
- ⅓ yard blue tonal
- ⅓ yard light green tonal
- ⅜ yard dark green tonal
- ½ yard bright yellow tonal
- ½ yard yellow tonal
- ½ yard bright blue tonal
- ⅝ yard red tonal
- ¾ yard navy tonal
- 1½ yards white print
- Batting 58" x 64"
- Backing 58" x 64"
- Neutral-color all-purpose thread
- Invisible quilting thread
- Basic sewing tools and supplies

Cutting
1. Cut three 2½" by fabric width A strips bright blue tonal.

2. Cut one 6½" by fabric width strip bright blue tonal; subcut strip into six 6½" F squares.

3. Cut three 2½" by fabric width B strips white print.

4. Cut two 3⅞" strips white print; subcut strips into (16) 3⅞" H squares.

5. Cut one 7¼" by fabric width strip white print; subcut strip into four 7¼" squares. Cut each square on both diagonals to make 16 M triangles.

6. Cut one 6½" by fabric width strip white print; subcut strip into eight 2½" x 6½" O rectangles.

House of White Birches, Berne, Indiana 46711 Clotilde.com

7. Cut five 3½" by fabric width S strips white print.

8. Cut one 3½" by fabric width strip yellow tonal; subcut strip into four 3½" C squares.

9. Cut one 6⅞" by fabric width strip yellow tonal; subcut strip into five 6⅞" J squares.

10. Cut two 3½" by fabric width strips red tonal; subcut strips into (16) 3½" D squares.

11. Cut two 3⅞" by fabric width strips red tonal; subcut strips into (16) 3⅞" I squares.

12. Cut one 3½" by fabric width strip dark green tonal; subcut strip into (12) 3½" E squares.

13. Cut one 6½" by fabric width strip dark green tonal; subcut strip into eight 2½" x 6½" N rectangles.

14. Cut two 2½" by fabric width strips bright yellow tonal; subcut strips into (24) 2½" G squares.

15. Cut one 6½" by fabric width strip bright yellow tonal; subcut strip into eight 2½" x 6½" P rectangles.

16. Cut one 6⅞" by fabric width strip blue tonal; subcut strip into five 6⅞" K squares.

17. Cut one 7¼" by fabric width strip light green tonal; subcut strip into four 7¼" squares. Cut each square on both diagonals to make 16 L triangles.

18. Cut five 1½" by fabric width Q/R strips navy tonal.

19. Cut six 2¼" by fabric width strips navy tonal for binding.

Completing the Nine-Patch Blocks

1. Sew a B strip between two A strips to make an A-B-A strip set; press seams toward A strips.

2. Subcut the A-B-A strip set into eight 2½" A-B-A segments as shown in Figure 1.

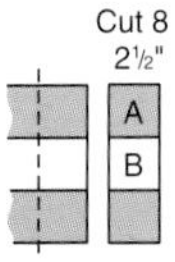

Cut 8
2½"

Figure 1

3. Sew an A strip between two B strips to make a B-A-B strip set; press seams toward A strip.

4. Subcut the B-A-B strip set into (16) 2½" B-A-B segments as shown in Figure 2.

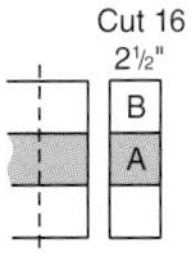

Cut 16
2½"

Figure 2

5. Sew a B-A-B segment to opposite sides of one A-B-A segment to complete one Nine-Patch block referring to Figure 3; press seams in one direction.

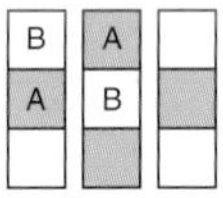

Figure 3

6. Repeat step 5 to make a total of eight Nine-Patch blocks.

Completing the Yellow Four-Patch Blocks

1. Sew a C square to a D square to make a row as shown in Figure 4; press seam toward D. Repeat to make four rows.

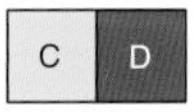

Figure 4

2. Select and join two rows to complete one Yellow Four-Patch block referring to Figure 5; press seam to one side.

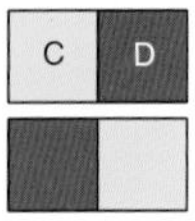

Figure 5

3. Repeat step 2 to complete a second Yellow Four-Patch block.

Completing the Green Four-Patch Blocks

1. Sew an E square to a D square to make a row as shown in Figure 6; press seam toward D. Repeat to make 12 rows.

Figure 6

2. Select and join two rows to complete one Green Four-Patch block referring to Figure 7; press seam to one side.

Figure 7

3. Repeat step 2 to complete a total of six Green Four-Patch blocks.

Completing the Snowball Blocks

1. Draw a diagonal line from corner to corner on the wrong side of each G square.

2. To complete one Snowball block, place a marked G square right sides together on each corner of one F square and stitch on the marked lines as shown in Figure 8.

Figure 8

3. Trim seam allowance to ¼" on each stitched corner as shown in Figure 9; press G pieces to the right side to complete one block, again referring to Figure 9.

Figure 9

4. Repeat steps 2 and 3 to complete a total of six Snowball blocks.

Completing the Pinwheel Blocks

1. Draw a diagonal line from corner to corner on the wrong side of each H square.

2. Place a marked H square right sides together with an I square and stitch ¼" on each side of the marked line as shown in Figure 10.

Figure 10

3. Cut the stitched unit in half on the marked line to make two H-I units as shown in Figure 11; press seams toward I.

Figure 11

4. Repeat steps 2 and 3 to make a total of 32 H-I units.

5. To make one Pinwheel block, select four H-I units. Join two units to make a row as shown in Figure 12; repeat to make a second row. Press seam to one side.

Figure 12

6. Join the two rows to complete one Pinwheel block as shown in Figure 13; press seams in one direction.

Figure 13

7. Repeat steps 5 and 6 to complete a total of eight Pinwheel blocks.

Completing the Half-Square Triangle Blocks

1. Draw a diagonal line from corner to corner on the wrong side of each J square.

2. Place a J square right sides together with a K square and stitch ¼" on each side of the marked line as shown in Figure 14.

Figure 14

3. Cut the stitched unit apart on the marked line to complete two Half-Square Triangle blocks as shown in Figure 15.

Figure 15

4. Repeat steps 2 and 3 to complete a total of 10 Half-Square Triangle blocks.

Completing the Hourglass Blocks

1. To complete one Hourglass block, select two each L and M triangles.

2. Sew L to M on one short side to make an L-M unit as shown in Figure 16; press seam toward L. Repeat to make a second L-M unit.

Figure 16

3. Join the two L-M units as shown in Figure 17 to complete one Hourglass block; press seam to one side.

Figure 17

4. Repeat steps 1–3 to complete a total of eight Hourglass blocks.

Completing the Rail Fence Blocks

1. To complete one Rail Fence block, select one each N, O and P rectangle.

2. Join the rectangles in alphabetical order as shown in Figure 18 to complete one Rail Fence block; press seams in one direction.

Figure 18

3. Repeat steps 1 and 2 to complete a total of eight Rail Fence blocks.

Completing the Quilt Top

1. Arrange and join the blocks in eight rows of seven blocks each referring to Figure 19 for positioning of blocks in rows; press seams in adjoining rows in opposite directions.

2. Join the rows to complete the pieced center, again referring to Figure 19 and the Placement Diagram for positioning of rows; press seams in one direction.

Figure 19

3. Join the Q/R strips on short ends to make one long strip; press seams open. Subcut strip into two 1½" x 48½" Q strips and two 1½" x 44½" R strips.

4. Sew a Q strip to opposite sides and R strips to the top and bottom of the pieced center; press seams toward Q and R strips.

5. Join the S strips on short ends to make one long strip; press seams open. Subcut strip into four 3½" x 50½" S strips.

6. Sew S strips to opposite sides and then to the top and bottom of the pieced center to complete the quilt top; press seams toward the S strips.

Completing the Quilt

1. Sandwich the batting between the pieced quilt top and the prepared backing piece; pin or baste layers together to hold. Quilt as desired by hand or machine.

2. When quilting is complete, trim batting and backing fabric even with raw edges of the quilt top.

3. Join previously cut binding strips on short ends with diagonal seams to make one long strip as shown in Figure 20; trim seams to ¼" and press seams open.

Figure 20

4. Fold the binding strip with wrong sides together along length; press.

5. Sew binding to the quilt edges, mitering corners and overlapping ends. Fold binding to the back side and stitch in place to finish the quilt. ■

Sweet & Simple Sampler
Placement Diagram 50" x 56"

Baby Blocks

This quilt would look wonderful with any bright and fun novelty print. It's a quick and easy project that's the perfect gift for the next baby shower you attend.

Project Specifications
Skill Level: Beginner
Quilt Size: 45" x 54"
Block Size: 9" x 9"
Number of Blocks: 10

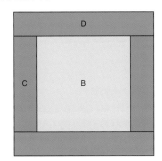

Baby Block
9" x 9" Block
Make 10

Materials
- 10 precut 2" by fabric width C/D strips assorted tonals to coordinate with the novelty print
- ⅓ yard green tonal
- ½ yard green solid
- ⅔ yard white tonal
- 1⅜ yards novelty print
- Batting 53" x 62"
- Backing 53" x 62"
- Neutral-color all-purpose thread
- Invisible quilting thread
- Basic sewing tools and supplies

Cutting
1. Cut three 9½" by fabric width strips novelty print; subcut strips into (10) 9½" A squares.

2. Cut two 6½" by fabric width strips novelty print; subcut strips into (10) 6½" B squares.

3. Cut three 1½" by fabric width E strips green tonal.

4. Cut two 1½" x 38½" F strips green tonal.

5. Cut five 4" by fabric width G/H strips white tonal.

6. Cut five 2¼" by fabric width strips green solid for binding.

7. Cut each C/D strip into two 2" x 6½" C strips and two 2" x 9½" D strips.

Completing the Blocks
1. Select one B square and two each matching C and D strips to complete one Baby Block.

2. Sew a C strip to opposite sides of the B square to make a B-C unit as shown in Figure 1; press seams toward C strips. *Note: If the novelty fabric is directional, be sure the C strips are stitched to the sides of the upright square.*

Figure 1

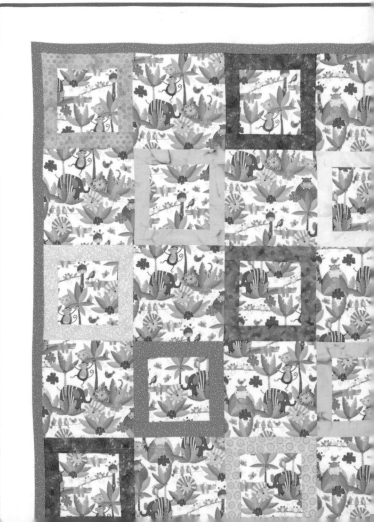

3. Sew a D strip to the top and bottom of the B-C unit to complete one Baby Block referring to Figure 2; press seams toward D strips.

Figure 2

4. Repeat steps 1–3 to complete a total of 10 Baby Block blocks.

Completing the Quilt Top

1. Select and join two Baby Blocks and two A squares to make a row as shown in Figure 3; press seams toward A. Repeat to make five rows. *Note: If the novelty print is directional, refer to the Placement Diagram for positioning of blocks in each row; rows may not be pieced and turned in alternating rows.*

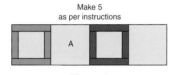

Make 5
as per instructions

Figure 3

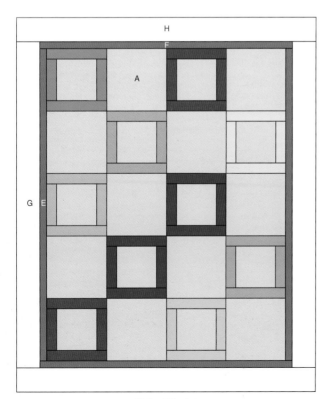

Baby Blocks
Placement Diagram 45" x 54"

2. Join the rows referring to the Placement Diagram to complete the pieced center; press seams in one direction.

3. Join the E strips on the short ends to make one long strip; press seams open. Subcut strip into two 1½" x 45½" E strips.

4. Sew an E strip to opposite long sides and F strips to the top and bottom of the pieced center; press seams toward E and F strips.

5. Join the G/H strips on short ends to make a long strip; press seams open. Subcut strip into two 4" x 47½" G strips and two 4" x 45½" H strips.

6. Sew a G strip to opposite long sides and H strips to the top and bottom of the pieced center to complete the quilt top; press seams toward G and H strips.

Completing the Quilt

1. Sandwich the batting between the pieced quilt top and the prepared backing piece; pin or baste layers together to hold. Quilt as desired by hand or machine.

2. When quilting is complete, trim batting and backing fabric even with raw edges of the quilt top.

3. Join previously cut binding strips on short ends with diagonal seams to make one long strip as shown in Figure 4; trim seams to ¼" and press seams open.

Figure 4

4. Fold the binding strip with wrong sides together along length; press.

5. Sew binding to the quilt edges, mitering corners and overlapping ends. Fold binding to the back side and stitch in place to finish the quilt. ■

Here's My Heart

Give a piece of your heart to someone you love.
Any young lady would appreciate this quilt in her bedroom.

Project Specifications
Skill Level: Beginner
Quilt Size: 53⅝" x 53⅝"
Block Size: 4½" x 4½"
Number of Blocks: 56

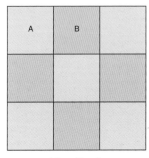

Nine-Patch
4½" x 4½" Block
Make 24

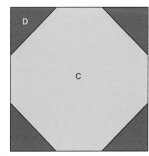

Snowball
4½" x 4½" Block
Make 32

Materials
• ¼ yard light rose tonal
• ½ yard light green tonal
• ⅝ yard light blue tonal
• ⅔ yard pink print
• ⅔ yard pink heart print
• 1 yard blue floral
• 1¼ yards dark pink tonal
• Batting 62" x 62"
• Backing 62" x 62"
• Neutral-color all-purpose thread
• Light pink quilting thread
• Basic sewing tools and supplies

Cutting
1. Cut eight 2" by fabric with A strips light blue tonal.

2. Cut seven 2" by fabric width B strips light green tonal.

3. Cut four 5" by fabric width strips pink print; subcut strips into (32) 5" C squares.

4. Cut seven 2" by fabric width strips dark pink tonal; subcut strips into (128) 2" D squares.

5. Cut five 1½" by fabric width I/J strips dark pink tonal.

6. Cut six 2¼" by fabric width strips dark pink tonal for binding.

7. Cut one 5" by fabric width strip light rose tonal; subcut strip into eight 5" F squares.

8. Cut two 7⅝" by fabric width strips blue floral; subcut strips into six 7⅝" squares. Cut each square on both diagonals to make 24 G triangles.

9. Cut the remainder of a 7⅝" strip into two 4⅛" squares. Cut each square in half on one diagonal to make a total of four H triangles.

10. Cut three 5" by fabric width strips blue floral; subcut strips into (21) 5" E squares.

11. Cut five 4" by fabric width K/L strips pink heart print.

Completing the Nine-Patch Blocks
1. Sew an A strip to opposite sides of a B strip with right sides together along length to make an A-B-A strip set; press seams toward A strips. Repeat to make a total of three A-B-A strip sets.

2. Subcut the A-B-A strip sets into (48) 2" A-B-A segments as shown in Figure 1.

Figure 1

3. Sew a B strip to opposite sides of an A strip with right sides together along length to make a B-A-B strip set; press seams toward the A strip. Repeat to make a second B-A-B strip set.

4. Subcut the B-A-B strip sets into (24) 2" B-A-B segments as shown in Figure 2.

Figure 2

5. Select and sew an A-B-A segment to opposite sides of a B-A-B segment to complete one Nine-Patch block referring to Figure 3; press seams in one direction.

Figure 3

6. Repeat step 5 to complete a total of 24 Nine-Patch blocks.

Completing the Snowball Blocks

1. Draw a diagonal line from corner to corner on the wrong side of each D square.

2. To complete one Snowball block, select one C square and four marked D squares.

3. Place a D square right sides together on each corner of the C square and stitch on the marked line as shown in Figure 4.

Figure 4

4. Trim seam allowance to ¼" and press D to the right side to complete one Snowball block as shown in Figure 5.

Figure 5

5. Repeat steps 2–4 to complete a total of 32 Snowball blocks.

Completing the Quilt Top

1. Sew a G triangle to opposite sides of a Nine-Patch block and add an H triangle to make a corner unit as shown in Figure 6; press seams toward G and H. Repeat to make a second corner unit.

Corner Unit
Make 2

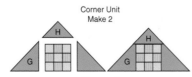

Figure 6

2. Arrange and join the remaining Nine-Patch blocks, and G and H triangles with the Snowball blocks, and the E and F squares in diagonal rows as shown in Figure 7. Press seams in adjacent rows in opposite directions.

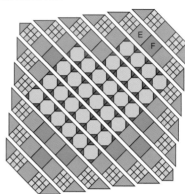

Figure 7

3. Join the rows and add corner units as shown in Figure 8 to complete the pieced center; press seams in one direction.

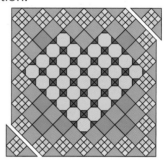

Figure 8

4. Join the I/J strips on the short ends to make one long strip; press seams open. Subcut strip into two 1½" x 45⅛" I strips and two 1½" x 47⅛" J strips.

5. Sew an I strip to opposite sides and J strips to the top and bottom of the pieced center; press seams toward I and J strips.

6. Join the K/L strips on short ends to make one long strip; press seams open. Subcut strip into two 4" x 47⅛" K strips and two 4" x 54⅛" L strips.

7. Sew a K strip to opposite sides and L strips to the top and bottom of the pieced center to complete the quilt top; press seams toward K and L strips.

Completing the Quilt

1. Sandwich the batting between the pieced quilt top and the prepared backing piece; pin or baste layers together to hold. Quilt as desired by hand or machine.

2. When quilting is complete, trim batting and backing fabric even with raw edges of the quilt top.

3. Join previously cut binding strips on short ends with diagonal seams to make one long strip as shown in Figure 9; trim seams to ¼" and press seams open.

Figure 9

4. Fold the binding strip with wrong sides together along length; press.

5. Sew binding to the quilt edges, mitering corners and overlapping ends. Fold binding to the back side and stitch in place to finish the quilt. ■

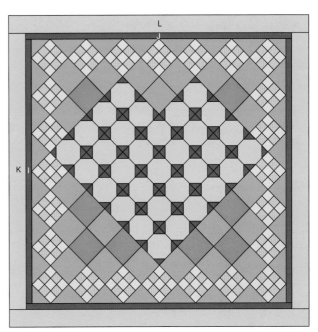

Here's My Heart
Placement Diagram 53⅝" x 53⅝"

Let's Go

Any young boy would love playing on this bright and fun quilt—a quilt made for daydreams.

Project Specifications
Skill Level: Beginner
Quilt Size: 37½" x 43½"
Block Size: 6" x 6"
Number of Blocks: 15

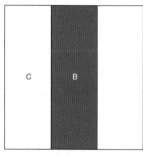

Red Rail Fence
6" x 6" Block
Make 6

Dark Green Rail Fence
6" x 6" Block
Make 5

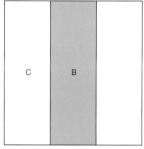

Light Green Rail Fence
6" x 6" Block
Make 4

Materials
- 1 fat quarter each 5 different vehicle or travel-related novelty prints
- ⅛ yard each red, light green and dark green tonals
- ¼ yard black solid
- ½ yard truck print
- ½ yard blue solid
- ⅝ yard white multicolored dot
- Batting 46" x 52"
- Backing 46" x 52"
- Neutral-color all-purpose thread
- Invisible quilting thread
- Basic sewing tools and supplies

Cutting
1. Cut one 6½" x 21" strip each fat quarter; subcut each strip into three 6½" A squares.

2. Cut one 2½" by fabric width B strip each red, light green and dark green tonals.

3. Cut six 2½" by fabric width C strips white multi-colored dot.

4. Cut two 1¼" x 36½" D strips and two 1¼" x 32" E strips black solid.

5. Cut four 3½" x 38" F strips truck print.

6. Cut five 2¼" by fabric width strips blue solid for binding.

Completing the Blocks
1. Sew a B strip between two C strips with right sides together along length to make a B-C strip set; press seams toward B.

2. Repeat to make a total of three B-C strip sets—one each red, light green and dark green.

3. Subcut each strip set into 6½" B-C segments to complete six Red Rail Fence, four Light Green Rail Fence and five Dark Green Rail Fence blocks as shown in Figure 1.

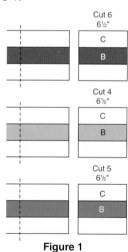

Figure 1

Completing the Quilt Top

1. Select and join three A squares and two Red Rail Fence blocks to make Row 1 as shown in Figure 2; press seams toward A. *Note: Be careful to orient A squares in an upright position in the rows if fabrics are directional.*

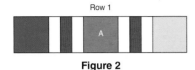

Figure 2

2. Select and join one Light Green Rail Fence block, two A squares and two Dark Green Rail Fence blocks to make Row 2 as shown in Figure 3; press seams toward A.

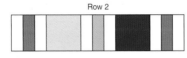

Figure 3

3. Select and join three A squares and one each Light Green and Dark Green Rail Fence block to make Row 3 as shown in Figure 4; press seams toward A.

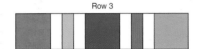

Figure 4

4. Select and join two A squares, two Red Rail Fence blocks and one Light Green Rail Fence block to make Row 4 as shown in Figure 5; press seams toward A.

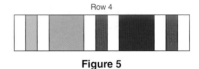

Figure 5

5. Select and join three A squares and one each Light Green and Dark Green Rail Fence block to make Row 5 as shown in Figure 6; press seams toward A.

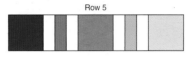

Figure 6

6. Select and join two A squares, two Red Rail Fence blocks and one Dark Green Rail Fence block to make Row 6 as shown in Figure 7; press seams toward A.

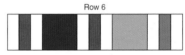

Figure 7

7. Arrange and join the rows in numerical order to complete the pieced center referring to the Placement Diagram for positioning of rows; press seams in one direction.

8. Sew a D strip to opposite long sides and E strips to the top and bottom of the pieced center; press seams toward D and E strips.

9. Sew F strips to opposite long sides and to the top and bottom of the pieced center to complete the quilt top; press seams toward F strips.

Completing the Quilt

1. Sandwich the batting between the pieced quilt top and the prepared backing piece; pin or baste layers together to hold. Quilt as desired by hand or machine.

2. When quilting is complete, trim batting and backing fabric even with raw edges of the quilt top.

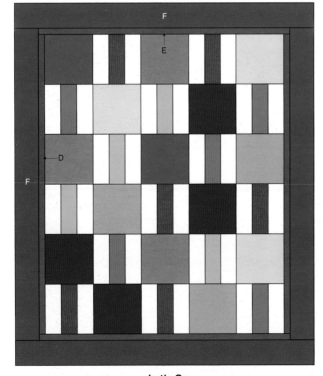

Let's Go
Placement Diagram 37½" x 43½"

3. Join previously cut binding strips on short ends with diagonal seams to make one long strip as shown in Figure 8; trim seams to ¼" and press seams open.

¼"

Figure 8

4. Fold the binding strip with wrong sides together along length; press.

5. Sew binding to the quilt edges, mitering corners and overlapping ends. Fold binding to the back side and stitch in place to finish the quilt. ■

Critters & Crawlers

A simple Square-in-a-Square block would make a great
I-Spy quilt, or it could showcase a child's favorite things.

Project Specifications
Skill Level: Beginner
Quilt Size: 44" x 56"
Block Size: 6" x 6"
Number of Blocks: 48

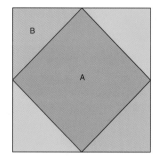

Square-in-a-Square
6" x 6" Block
Make 48

Materials
- Novelty prints—48 assorted 4¾" A squares
  or (6) 4¾" x 42" strips
- Bright-color tonals—96 pairs matching
  3⅞" B squares or (10) 3⅞" x 42" strips
- ⅓ yard navy tonal
- 1⅛ yards blue tonal
- Batting 52" x 64"
- Backing 52" x 62"
- Neutral-color all-purpose thread
- Invisible quilting thread
- Basic sewing tools and supplies

Cutting
1. If using 4¾" x 42" novelty print strips, subcut
strips into (48) 4¾" A squares.

2. If using 3⅞" x 42" bright-color tonal strips,
subcut strips into (96) 3⅞" B squares. Cut each B
square (from strip or precut squares) in half on one
diagonal to make a total of 192 B triangles, keeping
matching pairs of triangles together.

3. Cut three 1½" by fabric width C strips navy tonal.

4. Cut two 1½" x 38½" D strips navy tonal.

5. Cut five 3½" by fabric width E/F strips blue tonal.

6. Cut six 2¼" by fabric width strips blue tonal
for binding.

Completing the Blocks
1. To complete one Square-in-a-Square block,
select one A square and two sets of two matching
B triangles.

2. Sew a matching B triangle to opposite sides of
the A square as shown in Figure 1; press seams
toward B.

Figure 1

3. Sew the remaining two matching B triangles to
the remaining sides of A to complete one Square-
in-a-Square block referring to Figure 2.

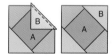

Figure 2

4. Repeat steps 1–3 to complete a total of 48
Square-in-a-Square blocks.

Completing the Quilt Top
1. Select and join six Square-in-a-Square blocks to
make a row; press seams in one direction. Repeat
to make a total of eight rows.

2. Join the rows with seams pressed in opposite
directions to complete the pieced center; press
seams in one direction.

3. Join the C strips on short ends to make one long
strip; press seams open. Subcut strip into two 1½" x
48½" C strips.

4. Sew C strips to opposite long sides and D strips
to the top and bottom of the pieced center; press
seams toward C and D strips.

5. Join the E/F strips on short ends to make one long strip; press seams open. Subcut strip into two 3½" x 50½" E strips and two 3½" x 44½" F strips.

6. Sew E strips to opposite long sides and F strips to the top and bottom of the pieced center to complete the quilt top; press seams toward E and F strips.

Completing the Quilt

1. Sandwich the batting between the pieced quilt top and the prepared backing piece; pin or baste layers together to hold. Quilt as desired by hand or machine.

2. When quilting is complete, trim batting and backing fabric even with raw edges of the quilt top.

3. Join previously cut binding strips on short ends with diagonal seams to make one long strip as shown in Figure 3; trim seams to ¼" and press seams open.

Figure 3

4. Fold the binding strip with wrong sides together along length; press.

5. Sew binding to the quilt edges, mitering corners and overlapping ends. Fold binding to the back side and stitch in place to finish the quilt. ■

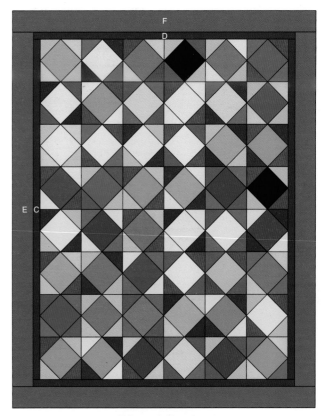

Critters & Crawlers
Placement Diagram 44" x 56"

Check This!

Choose a novelty fabric and use up your scraps and make this adorable baby quilt. There are so many possibilities with this fast and easy design.

Project Specifications
Skill Level: Beginner
Quilt Size: 42" x 60"

Materials
- 162 assorted 2½" A squares in light, medium and dark fabrics to coordinate with novelty print
- ⅝ yard coordinating binding fabric
- ⅝ yard coordinating border fabric
- 1¾ yards novelty print
- Batting 50" x 68"
- Backing 50" x 68"
- Neutral-color all-purpose thread
- Invisible quilting thread
- Basic sewing tools and supplies

Cutting
1. Cut six 2¼" by fabric width strips coordinating binding fabric.

2. Cut five 3½" by fabric width C/D strips coordinating border fabric.

3. Cut four 6½" x 54½" B strips along the length of the novelty print.

Completing the Quilt Top
1. Select 27 A squares. Arrange and join to make an A strip as shown in Figure 1; press seams in one direction. Repeat to make a total of six A strips.

Figure 1

2. Join two A strips to make a double A strip as shown in Figure 2; press seam to one side. Repeat to make a total of three double A strips.

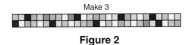

Figure 2

3. Join the double A strips with the B strips, beginning and ending with a B strip, to complete the pieced center; press seams toward A strips.

4. Join C/D strips on short ends to make a long strip; press seams open. Subcut strip into two 3½" x 54½" C strips and two 3½" x 42½" D strips.

5. Sew C strips to opposite long sides and D strips to the top and bottom of the pieced center to complete the quilt top.

Completing the Quilt

1. Sandwich the batting between the pieced quilt top and the prepared backing piece; pin or baste layers together to hold. Quilt as desired by hand or machine.

2. When quilting is complete, trim batting and backing fabric even with raw edges of the quilt top.

3. Join previously cut binding strips on short ends with diagonal seams to make one long strip as shown in Figure 3; trim seams to ¼" and press seams open.

Figure 3

4. Fold the binding strip with wrong sides together along length; press.

5. Sew binding to the quilt edges, mitering corners and overlapping ends. Fold binding to the back side and stitch in place to finish the quilt. ∎

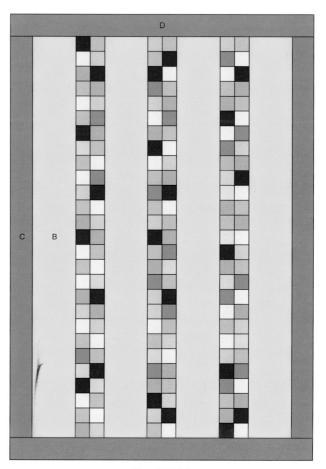

Check This!
Placement Diagram 42" x 60"

Chevron Points

Make a cute Log Cabin variation quilt in a day. Any theme would work well with this design. Pick a fun fabric, and the rest is a breeze.

Project Specifications
Skill Level: Beginner
Quilt Size: 47½" x 47½"
Block Size: 8½" x 8½"
Number of Blocks: 13

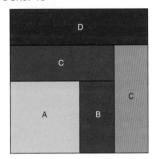

Chevron Log Cabin
8½" x 8½" Block
Make 13

Materials
- 12 precut 2½" x 42" strips assorted light and dark brown tonals
- ½ yard cream tonal
- ¾ yard blue tonal
- 1⅛ yards cowboy print
- Batting 56" x 56"
- Backing 56" x 56"
- Neutral-color all-purpose thread
- Invisible quilting thread
- Basic sewing tools and supplies

Cutting
1. Cut two 5" by fabric width strips cowboy print; subcut strips into (13) 5" A squares.

2. Cut two 4½" x 40" I strips cowboy print.

3. Cut three 4½" by fabric width J strips cowboy print.

4. Cut one 14" by fabric width strip cream tonal; subcut strip into two 14" squares and two 7⅝" squares. Cut the 14" squares on both diagonals to make eight E triangles. Cut the 7⅝" squares in half on one diagonal to make four F triangles.

5. Cut two 2" x 37" G strips and two 2" x 40" H strips blue tonal.

6. Cut five 2¼" by fabric width strips blue tonal for binding.

7. Cut the 2½" precut strips into the following sizes: (13) 2½" x 5" B strips, (26) 2½" x 7" C strips, and (13) 2½" x 9" D strips.

Completing the Blocks
1. To complete one Chevron Log Cabin block, select one each A square, B strip and D strip, and two C strips.

2. Sew a B strip to the A square as shown in Figure 1; press seam toward B.

Figure 1

3. Sew a C strip to the top and a second C strip to the B side of the A-B unit referring to Figure 2; press seam toward C strips.

Figure 2

4. Sew a D strip to the top of the pieced unit to complete one Chevron Log Cabin block referring to Figure 3; press seam toward D.

Figure 3

5. Repeat steps 1–4 to complete a total of 13 Chevron Log Cabin blocks.

Completing the Quilt Top
1. Select one Chevron Log Cabin block, one F triangle and two E triangles.

2. Sew an E triangle to opposite sides and the F triangle to one side of the block, matching square ends of E triangles to the edges of the blocks and centering the F triangle as shown in Figure 4 to complete a corner unit; press seams toward E and F. *Note: The triangles are longer than the blocks so that the blocks will float on the background after piecing. Add the triangles to the blocks carefully, referring to Figures 4, 5, 9 and the Placement Diagram for positioning of blocks and triangles. It is important that the blocks are oriented properly.*

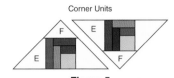

Figure 4

3. Repeat steps 1 and 2 to complete the opposite corner unit, again referring to Figure 5.

Corner Units

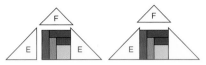

Figure 5

4. Select and join two E triangles and three Chevron Log Cabin blocks to make Row 1, extending the E triangles at one end as shown in Figure 6; press seams in one direction.

Figure 6

5. Select and join two F triangles and five Chevron Log Cabin blocks to make the center row, centering the F triangles at the ends as shown in Figure 7; press seams in the opposite direction from Row 1.

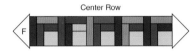

Figure 7

6. Select and join two E triangles and three Chevron Log Cabin blocks to make Row 3 as shown in Figure 8; press seams in the opposite direction from the center row.

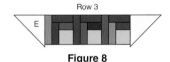

Figure 8

7. Arrange and join the rows and the corner units referring to Figure 9 to complete the pieced center; press seams in one direction.

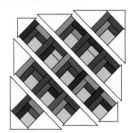

Figure 9

8. Trim the pieced center to 37" x 37", leaving an equal amount of the E and F triangles showing all around. *Note: The pieced section of the quilt top should appear to float on the triangle background pieces.*

9. Sew G strips to opposite sides and H strips to the top and bottom of the pieced center; press seams toward G and H strips.

10. Sew I strips to opposite sides of the pieced center; press seams toward I strips.

11. Join the J strips on the short ends to make one long strip; press seams open. Subcut strip into two 4½" x 48" J strips.

12. Sew a J strip to the top and bottom of the pieced center to complete the quilt top; press seams toward J strips.

Completing the Quilt

1. Sandwich the batting between the pieced quilt top and the prepared backing piece; pin or baste layers together to hold. Quilt as desired by hand or machine.

2. When quilting is complete, trim batting and backing fabric even with raw edges of the quilt top.

3. Join previously cut binding strips on short ends with diagonal seams to make one long strip as shown in Figure 10; trim seams to ¼" and press seams open.

Figure 10

4. Fold the binding strip with wrong sides together along length; press.

5. Sew binding to the quilt edges, mitering corners and overlapping ends. Fold binding to the back side and stitch in place to finish the quilt. ∎

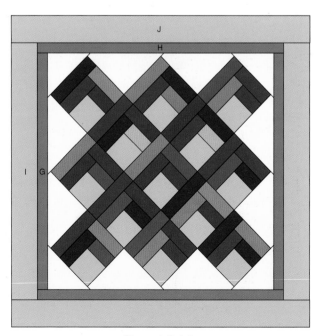

Chevron Points
Placement Diagram 47½" x 47½"

Leapin' Nine-Patch

Make nap time fun for any young child with this cute quilt wrapped around them.

Project Specifications
Skill Level: Beginner
Quilt Size: 42" x 48"
Block Size: 6" x 6"
Number of Blocks: 30

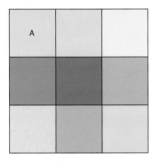

Nine-Patch
6" x 6" Block
Make 15

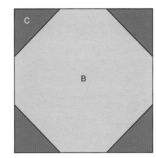

Light Blue Snowball
6" x 6" Block
Make 8

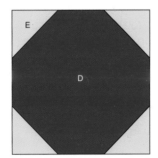

Dark Blue Snowball
6" x 6" Block
Make 7

Materials
Note: *Fabrics based on a 43" fabric width.*
- 9 assorted green and yellow precut 2½" A strips or cut 135 assorted green and yellow 2½" A squares
- ¼ yard yellow tonal
- ¼ yard green tonal
- ½ yard light blue novelty print
- ½ yard dark blue novelty print
- ⅔ yard dark green tonal
- ⅞ yard dark blue tonal
- Batting 50" x 56"
- Backing 50" x 56"
- Neutral-color all-purpose thread
- Invisible quilting thread
- Basic sewing tools and supplies

Cutting
1. If using strips for A, cut a total of (135) 2½" A squares from the strips.

2. Cut two 6½" by fabric width strips light blue novelty print; subcut strips into eight 6½" B squares.

3. Cut two 6½" by fabric width strips dark blue novelty print; subcut strips into seven 6½" D squares.

4. Cut two 2½" by fabric width strips green tonal; subcut strips into (32) 2½" C squares.

5. Cut two 2½" by fabric width strips yellow tonal; subcut strips into (28) 2½" E squares.

6. Cut four 2½" by fabric width strips dark blue tonal; trim strips to make two 2½" x 36½" F strips and two 2½" x 34½" G strips.

7. Cut four 3½" x 42½" J strips dark blue tonal.

8. Cut four 1½" by fabric width strips dark green tonal; trim strips to make two 1½" x 40½" H strips and two 1½" x 36½" I strips.

9. Cut five 2¼" by fabric width strips dark green tonal for binding.

Completing the Nine-Patch Blocks
1. To make one Nine-Patch block, randomly select nine A squares.

2. Join three A squares to make a row; press seams to one side. Repeat to make a total of three rows.

3. Arrange and join the rows with the seams in adjacent rows pressed in opposite directions to complete one Nine-Patch block as shown in Figure 1; press seams in one direction.

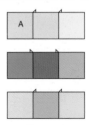

Figure 1

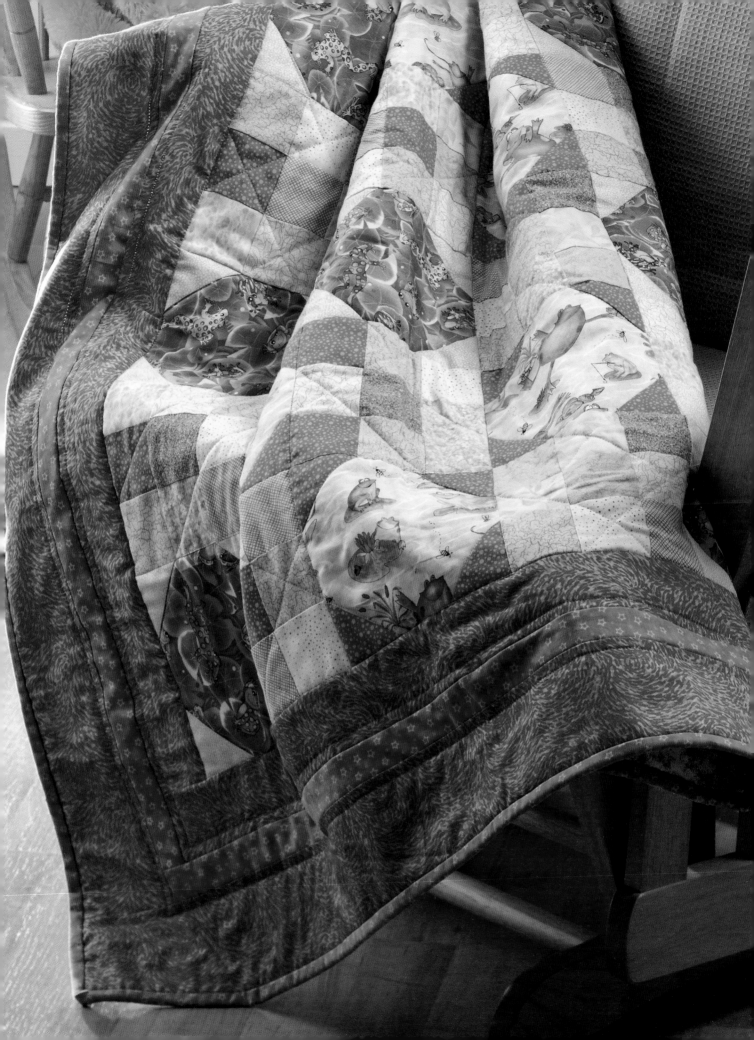

4. Repeat steps 1–3 to complete a total of 15 Nine-Patch blocks.

Completing the Snowball Blocks

1. Draw a diagonal line from corner to corner on the wrong side of each C and E square.

2. To complete one Light Blue Snowball block, select one B square and four marked C squares.

3. Place a C square on each corner of the B square and stitch on the marked lines as shown in Figure 2.

Figure 2

4. Trim seams to ¼" and press C to the right side to complete one Light Blue Snowball block as shown in Figure 3.

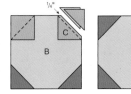

Figure 3

5. Repeat steps 2–4 to complete a total of eight Light Blue Snowball blocks.

6. Repeat steps 2–4 with the marked E squares and D squares as shown in Figure 4 to make a total of seven Dark Blue Snowball blocks.

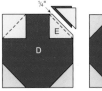

Figure 4

Completing the Quilt Top

1. Select and join two Light Blue Snowball blocks with three Nine-Patch blocks to make Row 1 as shown in Figure 5; press seams away from the Nine-Patch blocks. Repeat to make Rows 3 and 5. ***Note:*** *If the B and D fabrics are directional, pay close attention to the positioning of the squares in the rows.*

Make 3
Rows 1, 3 & 5

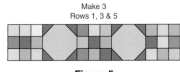

Figure 5

2. Select and join one Light Blue Snowball block and two each Nine-Patch and Dark Blue Snowball blocks to make Row 2 as shown in Figure 6; press seams away from the Nine-Patch blocks. Repeat to make Row 6.

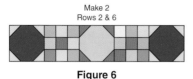

Make 2
Rows 2 & 6

Figure 6

3. Select and join two Nine-Patch blocks and three Dark Blue Snowball blocks to make Row 4 as shown in Figure 7; press seams away from the Nine-Patch blocks.

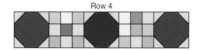

Row 4

Figure 7

4. Join the rows in numerical order to complete the pieced center referring to the Placement Diagram for positioning.

5. Sew F strips to opposite long sides and G strips to the top and bottom of the pieced center; press seams toward F and G strips.

6. Sew H strips to opposite long sides and I strips to the top and bottom of the pieced center; press seams toward H and I strips.

7. Sew J strips to opposite long sides and then to the top and bottom of the pieced center to complete the quilt top; press seams toward J strips.

Completing the Quilt

1. Sandwich the batting between the pieced quilt top and the prepared backing piece; pin or baste layers together to hold. Quilt as desired by hand or machine.

2. When quilting is complete, trim batting and backing fabric even with raw edges of the quilt top.

3. Join previously cut binding strips on short ends with diagonal seams to make one long strip as shown in Figure 8; trim seams to ¼" and press seams open.

Figure 8

4. Fold the binding strip with wrong sides together along length; press.

5. Sew binding to the quilt edges, mitering corners and overlapping ends. Fold binding to the back side and stitch in place to finish the quilt. ■

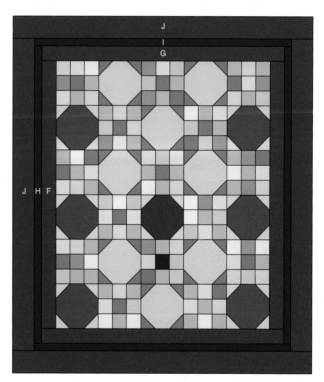

Leapin' Nine-Patch
Placement Diagram 42" x 48"

House of White Birches, Berne, Indiana 46711 Clotilde.com

Bugs

Bugs don't scare them! Toddlers will love investigating the interesting creepy-crawly bugs on this quilt.

Project Specifications
Skill Level: Beginner
Quilt Size: 45" x 54"
Block Size: 9" x 9"
Number of Blocks: 20

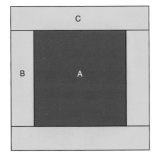

Blue Bugs
9" x 9" Block
Make 10

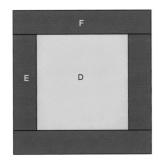

Yellow Bugs
9" x 9" Block
Make 10

Materials
- ⅝ yard blue tonal
- ¾ yard red tonal
- 1 yard blue bug print
- 1 yard yellow bug print
- Batting 53" x 62"
- Backing 53" x 62"
- Neutral-color all-purpose thread
- Variegated quilting thread
- Basic sewing tools and supplies

Cutting
1. Cut two 6½" by fabric width strips blue bug print; subcut strips into (10) 6½" A squares.

2. Cut one 6½" by fabric width strip blue bug print; subcut strip into (20) 2"x 6½" E strips.

3. Cut one 9½" by fabric width strip blue bug print; subcut strip into (20) 2" x 9½" F strips.

4. Cut two 6½" by fabric width strips yellow bug print; subcut strips into (10) 6½" D squares.

5. Cut one 6½" by fabric width strip yellow bug print; subcut strip into (20) 2" x 6½" B strips.

6. Cut one 9½" by fabric width strip yellow bug print; subcut strip into (20) 2" x 9½" C strips.

7. Cut five 2" by fabric width G strips red tonal.

8. Cut five 2¼" by fabric width strips red tonal for binding.

9. Cut five 3½" by fabric width H strips blue tonal.

Completing the Blocks
1. To complete one Blue Bugs block, select one A square and two each B and C strips.

2. Sew B strips to opposite sides and C strips to the top and bottom of the A square referring to Figure 1 to complete one Blue Bugs block; press seams toward B and C strips.

Figure 1

3. Repeat steps 1 and 2 to complete a total of 10 Blue Bugs blocks.

4. To complete one Yellow Bugs block, select one D square and two each E and F strips.

5. Sew E strips to opposite sides and F strips to the top and bottom of the D square referring to Figure 2 to complete one Yellow Bugs block; press seams toward E and F strips.

Figure 2

6. Repeat steps 4 and 5 to complete a total of 10 Yellow Bugs blocks.

Completing the Quilt Top

1. Select and join two each Yellow Bugs and Blue Bugs blocks to make a row as shown in Figure 3; press seams toward Yellow Bugs blocks. Repeat to make a total of five rows.

Make 5

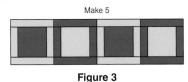

Figure 3

2. Join the rows, alternating placement referring to the Placement Diagram, to complete the pieced center; press seams in one direction.

3. Join the G strips on short ends to make one long strip; press seams open. Subcut strip into four 2" x 45½" G strips.

4. Join the H strips on short ends to make one long strip; press seams open. Subcut strip into four 3½" x 45½" H strips.

5. Sew a G strip to an H strip along the length to make a G-H strip; press seam toward G. Repeat to make a total of four G-H strips.

6. Sew a G-H strip to opposite sides and then to the top and bottom of the pieced center to complete the quilt top; press seams toward G-H strips.

Completing the Quilt

1. Sandwich the batting between the pieced quilt top and the prepared backing piece; pin or baste layers together to hold. Quilt as desired by hand or machine.

2. When quilting is complete, trim batting and backing fabric even with raw edges of the quilt top.

3. Join previously cut binding strips on short ends with diagonal seams to make one long strip as shown in Figure 4; trim seams to ¼" and press seams open.

Figure 4

4. Fold the binding strip with wrong sides together along length; press.

5. Sew binding to the quilt edges, mitering corners and overlapping ends. Fold binding to the back side and stitch in place to finish the quilt. ■

Bugs
Placement Diagram 45" x 54"

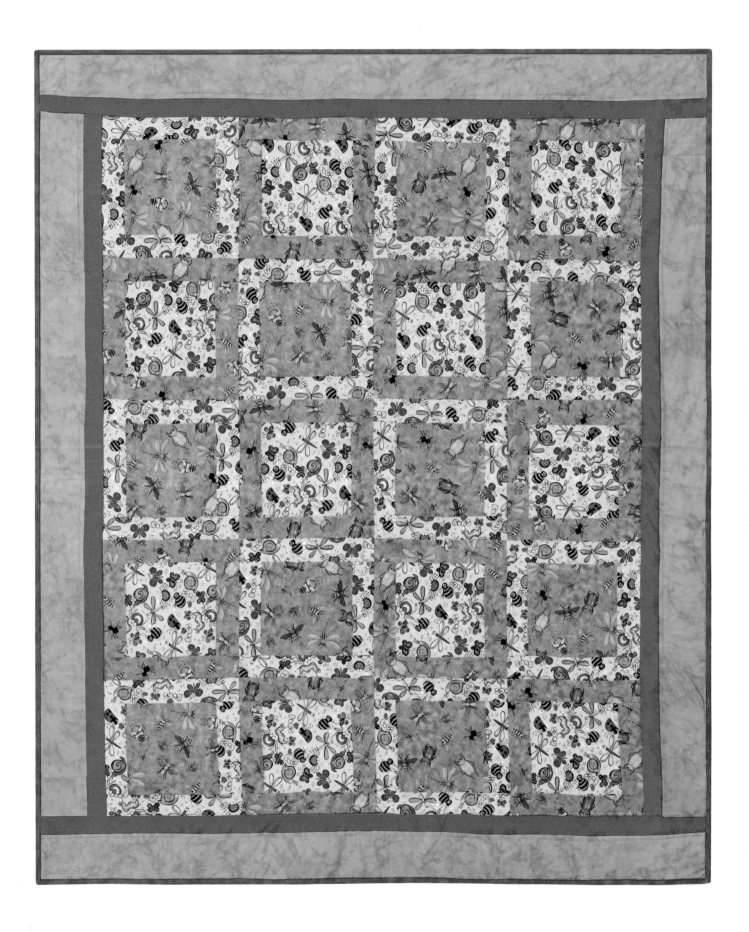

Baby Bricks

Do you have a lot of 2½" strips lying around your sewing room? Well, here's your opportunity to put them to good use—or you could use charm squares instead.

Project Specifications
Skill Level: Beginner
Quilt Size: 42" x 48"
Block Size: 6" x 6"
Number of Blocks: 42

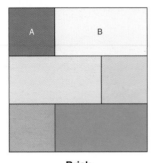

Brick
6" x 6" Block
Make 42

Materials
Note: *Yardage based on 43" usable fabric width.*
- 21 precut 2½" x 43" strips in assorted bright colors
- ⅞ yard bright blue tonal
- Batting 50" x 56"
- Backing 50" x 56"
- Neutral-color all-purpose thread
- Invisible quilting thread
- Basic sewing tools and supplies

Cutting
1. Cut six 2½" A squares and six 2½" x 4½" B rectangles from each precut strip to total 126 each A squares and B rectangles.

2. Cut four 3½" x 42½" C strips bright blue tonal.

3. Cut five 2¼" by fabric width strips bright blue tonal for binding.

Completing the Blocks
1. Sew an A square to a B rectangle to make an A-B unit as shown in Figure 1; press seam toward the darker fabric. Repeat to make a total of 126 A-B units, mixing up pieces to create a good variety.

Figure 1

2. To complete one Brick block, select and join three different A-B units referring to Figure 2; press seams in one direction.

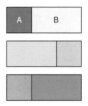

Figure 2

3. Repeat Step 2 to complete a total of 42 Brick blocks.

Completing the Quilt Top
1. Select six Brick blocks and join to make an X row, turning blocks when joining as shown in Figure 3; press seams to one side. Repeat to make four X rows. ***Note:*** *Pay attention to fabric placement to avoid the same fabrics meeting when blocks are joined.*

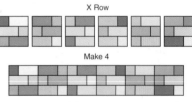

X Row
Make 4

Figure 3

2. Select six Brick blocks and join to make a Y row, positioning the blocks as shown in Figure 4; press seams to one side. Repeat to make three Y rows.

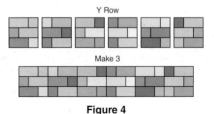

Y Row
Make 3

Figure 4

3. Arrange and join the rows referring to Figure 5 for positioning of rows, turning every other row to stagger pressed seams, to complete the pieced center; press seams in one direction.

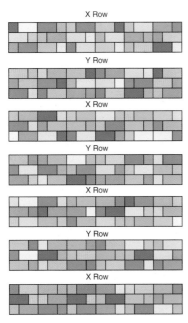

Figure 5

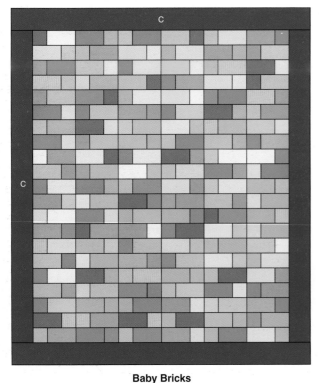

Baby Bricks
Placement Diagram 42" x 48"

4. Sew C strips to opposite sides and to the top and bottom of the pieced center; press seams toward C strips.

Completing the Quilt

1. Sandwich the batting between the pieced quilt top and the prepared backing piece; pin or baste layers together to hold. Quilt as desired by hand or machine.

2. When quilting is complete, trim batting and backing fabric even with raw edges of the quilt top.

3. Join previously cut binding strips on short ends with diagonal seams to make one long strip as shown in Figure 6; trim seams to ¼" and press seams open.

Figure 6

4. Fold the binding strip with wrong sides together along length; press.

5. Sew binding to the quilt edges, mitering corners and overlapping ends. Fold binding to the back side and stitch in place to finish the quilt. ■

Call of the Wild

Take a fun animal print and a few accent fabrics and you have a quilt that walks on the wild side.

Project Specifications

Skill Level: Beginner
Quilt Size: 44" x 50"
Block Size: 6" x 6"
Number of Blocks: 21

Strip Block
6" x 6" Block
Make 21

Materials

- ¼ yard each 5 different coordinating fabrics
- 21 assorted 6½" C squares or 5 fat quarters juvenile animal prints or ⅞ yard 1 print
- ½ yard gold tonal
- ½ yard black solid
- ¾ yard animal skin print
- Batting 52" x 58"
- Backing 52" x 58"
- Neutral-color all-purpose thread
- Invisible quilting thread
- Basic sewing tools and supplies

Cutting

1. Cut four 1½" by fabric width A strips from each of the five coordinating fabrics.

2. Cut four 1½" by fabric width B strips animal skin print.

3. Cut one 2½" by fabric width strip animal skin print; subcut strip into four 2½" H squares.

4. Cut five 2¼" by fabric width strips animal skin print for binding.

5. Cut three 2½" by fabric width F strips gold tonal.

6. Cut two 2½" x 38½" G strips gold tonal.

7. Cut two 1½" x 38½" E strips black solid.

8. Cut seven 1½" by fabric width D/I/J strips black solid.

9. If using yardage for C squares, cut four 6½" by fabric width strips animal print; subcut strips into (21) 6½" C squares. If using fat quarters for C squares, cut two 6½" x 21" strips from each of the five fat quarters. Subcut four sets of fat quarter strips into four 6½" C squares and one set of fat quarter strips into five 6½" C squares to total 21 C squares.

Completing the Blocks

1. Join one A strip from each coordinating fabric (five strips total) with one B strip to make a strip set; press seams in one direction. Repeat to make a total of four strip sets.

2. Subcut the strip set into (21) 6½" block segments as shown in Figure 1.

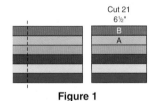

Figure 1

Completing the Quilt Top

1. Arrange and join three C squares with three Strip Blocks to make Row 1 as shown in Figure 2 (note position of B strips); press seams toward C squares. Repeat to make Row 5. **Note:** *If the C squares are cut from directional fabric, remember to keep them upright in each row.*

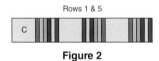

Figure 2

2. Arrange and join three C squares with three Strip Blocks to make Row 2 as shown in Figure 3; press seams toward C squares. Repeat to make row 6.

Rows 2 & 6

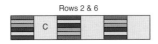

Figure 3

3. Arrange and join three C squares with three Strip Blocks to make Rows 3 and 7 referring to Figure 4; press seams toward C squares.

Rows 3 & 7

Figure 4

4. Arrange and join three C squares with three Strip Blocks to make Row 4 referring to Figure 5; press seams toward C squares.

Row 4

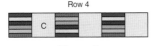

Figure 5

5. Arrange and join the rows in numerical order to complete the pieced center; press seams in one direction.

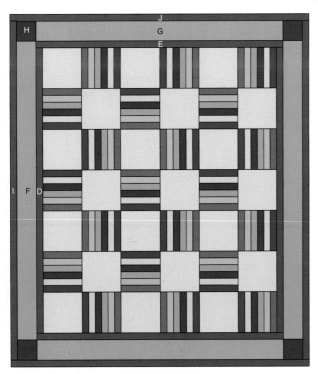

Call of the Wild
Placement Diagram 44" x 50"

6. Join the D/I/J strips on the short ends to make a long strip; press seams open. Subcut strip into two 1½" x 42½" D strips, two 1½" x 48½" I strips and two 1½" x 44½" J strips.

7. Sew D strips to opposite sides and E strips to the top and bottom of the pieced center; press seams toward D and E strips.

8. Join the F strips on the short ends to make a long strip; press seams open. Subcut strip into two 2½" x 44½" F strips.

9. Sew F strips to opposite sides of the pieced center; press seams toward F strips.

10. Sew an H square to each end of each G strip; press seams toward G.

11. Sew the G-H strips to the top and bottom of the pieced center; press seams toward G-H strips.

12. Sew I strips to opposite sides and J strips to the top and bottom of the pieced center to complete the quilt top; press seams toward I and J strips.

Completing the Quilt

1. Sandwich the batting between the pieced quilt top and the prepared backing piece; pin or baste layers together to hold. Quilt as desired by hand or machine.

2. When quilting is complete, trim batting and backing fabric even with raw edges of the quilt top.

3. Join binding strips on short ends with diagonal seams to make one long strip as shown in Figure 6; trim seams to ¼" and press seams open.

Figure 6

4. Fold the binding strip with wrong sides together along length; press.

5. Sew binding to the quilt edges, mitering corners and overlapping ends. Fold binding to the back side and stitch in place to finish the quilt. ■

Around the Block

Got a fun fabric with a lot of color? This pattern is perfect for that. Just keep adding borders.

Project Specifications
Skill Level: Beginner
Quilt Size: 43" x 58"

Materials
- Fat quarter orange tonal
- ⅝ yard blue tonal
- ⅞ yard novelty print
- 1⅛ yards yellow tonal
- 1⅛ yards green tonal
- Batting 51" x 66"
- Backing 51" x 66"
- Neutral-color all-purpose thread
- Invisible quilting thread
- Basic sewing tools and supplies

Cutting
1. Cut one 11½" x 26½" A rectangle novelty print.

2. Cut one 4½" by remaining fabric width strip novelty print; subcut strip into four 4½" G squares.

3. Cut two 2½" by fabric width strips yellow tonal; subcut each strip into one 2½" x 26½" B strip and one 2½" x 11½" C strip to total two each B and C strips.

4. Cut three 2½" by fabric width K strips yellow tonal.

5. Cut two 2½" x 31½" L strips yellow tonal.

6. Cut six 2¼" by fabric with strips yellow tonal for binding.

7. Cut one 2½" x 21" strip orange tonal; subcut strip into eight 2½" D squares.

8. Cut three 4½" by fabric width strips green tonal; subcut one strip into two 4½" x 15½" F strips and two 4½" J squares. Cut the remaining two strips to make two 4½" x 30½" E strips and two more 4½" J squares (four J squares total).

9. Cut two 4½" x 35½" N strips green tonal.

10. Cut three 4½" by fabric width M strips green tonal.

11. Cut four 4½" by fabric width strips blue tonal; subcut two strips to make two 4½" x 38½" H strips. Subcut each of the remaining strips into one

4½" x 23½" I strip and two 4½" O squares (to total two I strips and four O squares).

Completing the Quilt Top
1. Sew a B strip to opposite long sides of A as shown in Figure 1; press seams toward B.

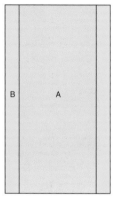

Figure 1

2. Sew a D square to each end of each C strip as shown in Figure 2 to make two C-D strips; press seams toward C strips.

Figure 2

3. Sew a C-D strip to the top and bottom of A-B; press seams toward C-D strips.

4. Referring to the Placement Diagram through step 15, sew an E strip to opposite long sides of the pieced unit; press seams toward E.

5. Sew a G square to each end of each F strip to make two F-G strips; press seams toward F strips.

6. Sew an F-G strip to the top and bottom of the pieced unit; press seams toward F-G strips.

7. Sew an H strip to opposite long sides of the pieced unit; press seams toward H.

8. Sew a J square to each end of each I strip to make two I-J strips; press seams toward I strips.

9. Sew an I-J strip to the top and bottom of the pieced unit; press seams toward I-J strips.

10. Join the K strips on short ends to make one long strip; press seams open. Subcut strip into two 2½" x 46½" K strips. Sew these strips to opposite long sides of the pieced unit; press seams toward K.

11. Sew a D square to each end of each L strip to make two D-L strips; press seams toward L strips.

12. Sew a D-L strip to the top and bottom of the pieced unit; press seams toward D-L strips.

13. Join the M strips on short ends to make one long strip; press seams open. Subcut strip into two 4½" x 50½" M strips. Sew these strips to opposite long sides of the pieced unit; press seams toward M.

14. Sew an O square to each end of each N strip to make two N-O strips; press seams toward N strips.

15. Sew an N-O strip to the top and bottom of the pieced unit to complete the quilt top; press seams toward N-O strips.

Completing the Quilt

1. Sandwich the batting between the pieced quilt top and the prepared backing piece; pin or baste layers together to hold. Quilt as desired by hand or machine.

2. When quilting is complete, trim batting and backing fabric even with raw edges of the runner top.

3. Join previously cut binding strips on short ends with diagonal seams to make one long strip as shown in Figure 3; trim seams to ¼" and press seams open.

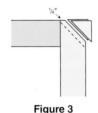

Figure 3

4. Fold the binding strip with wrong sides together along length; press.

5. Sew binding to the runner edges, mitering corners and overlapping ends. Fold binding to the back side and stitch in place to finish the quilt. ∎

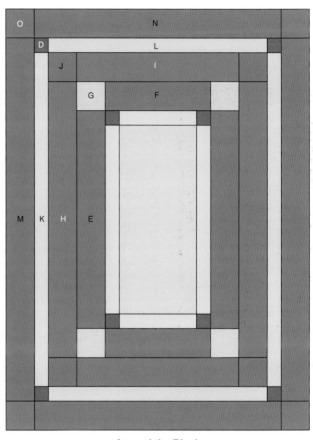

Around the Block
Placement Diagram 43" x 58"

HOUSE of
WHITE
BIRCHES
PUBLISHERS
SINCE 1947

Quick & Easy Quilts for Kids is published by DRG, 306 East Parr Road, Berne, IN 46711. Printed in USA. Copyright © 2012 DRG. All rights reserved. This publication may not be reproduced in part or in whole without written permission from the publisher.

RETAIL STORES: If you would like to carry this pattern book or any other DRG publications, visit DRGwholesale.com

Every effort has been made to ensure that the instructions in this pattern book are complete and accurate. We cannot, however, take responsibility for human error, typographical mistakes or variations in individual work. Please visit ClotildeCustomerCare.com to check for pattern updates.

ISBN: 978-1-59217-375-4
1 2 3 4 5 6 7 8 9